For Free Distribution

The Religious and Legal status of the Birthday
of the Beloved Prophet Muhammad ﷺ and
the concept of *Bid'ah*

Muslim Youth League
www.minhajuk.org

FOREWORD

∞

This booklet will discuss the legal and religious status of celebrating the birth of the Beloved Prophet Muhammad ﷺ, and the concept of *bid'ah* in light of the Qur'an and Sunnah. This is not a comprehensive guide since it is impossible to include all evidences in one concise booklet.

For a complete and comprehensive discourse on the validity of celebrating Mawlid-un-Nabi it is recommended to refer to Shaykh-ul-Islam. Dr. Muhammad Tahir-ul Qadri's book, *'Milad-un Nabi kee Sharee Haiseeyat'* and *'Mawlid-un-Nabi'*, DVD series in English.

Before you, however is an attempt to provide one with an insight to the topic and has been compiled from a series of lectures given by Shaykh-ul-Islam. Dr. Muhammad Tahir-ul-Qadri on this topic, which are available to listen to and are highly recommended both in English and Urdu.

This is a personal effort by the compilation team any mistakes that may occur in this compilation are of the compilation team alone thus we seek forgiveness from Almighty Allah for any errors that may occur.

PART ONE

The Religious and Legal status of
the Birthday of the Beloved Prophet
Muhammad ﷺ, in light of the Qur'an
and Sunnah

Ghazala Hasan Qadri

EVIDENCES FROM THE QUR'AN

∽

In the Qur'an, Allah 🕮 gives a clear order to celebrate and rejoice the raising and coming of the Beloved Prophet Muhammad 🕮. In Surah Yunus, Allah 🕮 states:

> *"Say: Because of the (fadl) Blessings of Allah 🕮 and His (rahma) Mercy you should celebrate (with happiness and pleasure). That is better than what (wealth) they amass."* [Qur'an 10:58]

In this particular verse Allah 🕮 is commanding that we should rejoice and celebrate His *fadl* (blessings) and *rahma* (mercy) as much as possible. The question naturally to be asked is what exactly should we be rejoicing? What does Allah's 🕮 *fadl* and *rahma* refer to? According to other verses in the Qur'an (*Tafsir bil Qur'an*) and the explanations given by scholars through their *Tafsir* works of this verse, the *fadl* and *rahma* in this verse is a direct reference to the Prophet Muhammad 🕮. He was sent to this world and His being raised for mankind is the greatest *fadl* and *rahma* of Allah 🕮, so we should all celebrate and rejoice this event.

There are many verses in the Qur'an where Allah 🕮 states that the Prophet Muhammad 🕮, is Allah's 🕮 *rahma* and *fadl*. In Surah Al Imran, Allah 🕮 states:

> *"Indeed Allah conferred a great **favour** on the believers when he sent among them a **Messenger** (Muhammad 🕮) from among themselves, reciting unto them His verses, and purifying them, and instructing them (in) the book and Al-Hikmah of the Prophet 🕮, while before that they had been in manifest error".* [Qur'an, 3:164]

In the Qur'an Allah 🕮 mentions the raising of Prophet Muhammad 🕮, as a favour, coming to mankind and providing humanity with the right path. His coming took people out of darkness and misguidance bringing them to the light of guidance and *Haq*. Allah 🕮 describes this as a great blessing by Him onto His people. Allah 🕮 states that if it had not been for His Beloved Prophet 🕮, we would all have been in a state of loss. Also Allah 🕮 uses the words *fadl* and *rahma* in the same sequence as in the verse of Surah Yunus thus denoting Allah's 🕮 *fadl* and *rahma* are indeed the Prophet Muhammad 🕮.

In Surah Al-Anbiya, Allah 🕮 describes the Prophet 🕮 as *rahma*:

"And We have sent you (oh Muhammad ﷺ) but as a Mercy for Mankind". [Qur'an, 21:107]

Here Prophet Muhammad ﷺ, has been given the name of *rahma*, it being one of his attributes. Imam Alusi in his tafsir, *Ruh ul Ma' ani* states that one of the glorious names of the Prophet ﷺ, is *rahma* even though his spiritual name is *Raheem*.

It is stated in Surah Al-Jumah,

"It is He who has sent among the unlettered ones a Messenger (Muhammad ﷺ) from among themselves, reciting to them His verse, purifying them, and teaching them the Book and Al-Hikama. And verily they had been in manifest error". [Qur'an, 62:2]

In this verse Allah ﷻ firstly lists all the qualities of the Prophet ﷺ and how he has taken mankind out of darkness. It is through his raising that we received guidance since divine revelation was given through Prophet Muhammad ﷺ in the form of the Qur'an. He inculcated us with knowledge and belief, and through his Sunnah we learnt how to implant it in our hearts and how to purify our inner selves according to the will and pleasure of Allah ﷻ. If the Prophet, ﷺ, had not been sent to us by Allah ﷻ then humanity would have remained misguided, in error and loss, and thus not be in position to receive anything from their Lord.

The verse addresses the people who lived in the time of the Prophet ﷺ, being sent "from among themselves". They were able to receive these great blessings directly from sitting with him, conversing with him, observing and receiving much from him. However Allah ﷻ does not confine this blessing and mercy to only those at the time of the Prophet ﷺ but states in the next verse

"And (He has sent him, Muhammad ﷺ, also to) others among them who have not yet joined them (but they will come). And He Allah is the Al-Mighty, the Wise." [Qur'an, 62:3]

Allah ﷻ confers His blessing not on only the Companions but on those who are yet to come. This is a reference to all future generations and is explicitly saying that the Prophet, ﷺ was not just a *fadl* for those in his time but for all generations to come. Thus there is no limit on the time period of when to rejoice. One may ask how it is possible that those who never saw or heard the Prophet, ﷺ, can still benefit from him? Yet that is up to Allah ﷻ and His wish and desire since He completes the verse by saying, *"Allah is the Almighty and Wise"*. He alone can do as He wishes and bestow what He wishes on whom He wants. There are no limits and boundaries on His power and if He wished for future generations to benefit from the *fadl* of the Prophet ﷺ, then so be it. So Allah's ﷻ raising of the Prophet ﷺ, is a *fadal of Allah*.

After explaining the extent and nature of His beloved Prophet's ﷺ mercy, then Allah ﷻ says in verse 4 of Surah Jumah:

*"That is the **Grace** of Allah, which He bestows on whom He wills. And Allah is the owner of Mighty Grace".* [Qur'an, 62:4]

"That is the Grace of Allah" is referring to the Prophet ﷺ, for he is the '*dhalika fadalullahi*', which has been described in verses 2 and 3. His being sent to the unlettered peoples providing wisdom is the Grace of Allah ﷻ.

An important point to note here is that the words later on in the verse, *"Allah is the owner of Mighty Grace"* are '*walla dhul fadl*'. This is a significant point since Allah ﷻ is the Lord of *fadl* but He Himself is not the *fadl*, which some commentators incorrectly translate as. He is the Lord of the highest blessing, its owner, its bestowal, and its possessor. For instance if you are an author of a book you are not the book itself. Similarly Allah ﷻ is *sahibul fadl*, its possessor. Allah ﷻ is not the favour itself as that is separate from the bestower. Then who is *fadl*? The Prophet Muhammad ﷺ, is the *fadl* given in verses 3 and 4. This is Allah's ﷻ bounty. The one who was raised by Him is the *fadl*.

In Arabic grammar the compound nouns, *muzaf* and *muzaf-ilai* are always different and can never be the same. For instance in the word *Rasulallah, rasul* is *muzaf* and Allah ﷻ is the *muzaf-ilai*. So in the words *Dhul fadl*, *fadl* is *muzaf* and Allah is the *muzafilai*, thus there can be no doubt that the *fadl* referred to here is Prophet Muhammad ﷺ.

In Surah Al-A'raf, it is stated:

> " ..My Mercy embraces all things. That (Mercy) I shall ordain for those who are Muttaqun, and give Zakah, and those who believe in Our evidences and signs". [Qur'an, 7:156]

So Allah's ﷻ *rahma* extends to all things, and he ordains this *rahma* on those who do right things, practice charity and follow the signs of Allah ﷻ. So who are these people entitled to this *rahma*? Who will do these practices? Allah ﷻ states in the next verse it is those who follow my messenger, who have been sent to the unlettered people. He is the *rahma* sent to them.

Thus from the above discussion it can be seen that Allah ﷻ has placed an *ehsan*, favour on us and in Surah Yunus we are expressly commanded to celebrate and rejoice this favour which is described as *rahma* and *fadl*. Other verses in the Qur'an explicitly define this *rahma* and *fadl* as referring to Prophet Muhammad ﷺ, thus celebrating his coming is a Divine command.

The Qur'an also singles out the birthday as an important event and worthy of mention. In Surah Maryam Allah ﷻ commands us to send *salaam* on the day Prophet Yahya عليه السلام was born i.e. his birthday.

*"And send salaam on him the day he was born,
and the day he dies and the day he will be raised
up to life (again)"* [Qur'an, 19:15]

The same commandment has also been given in
respect of Prophet Isa عليه السلام in Surah Maryam:

*"And send salaam on me the day I was born and
the day I died and the day I shall be raised alive"*
[Qur'an, 19:33]

If the celebration of birthdays is an innovation
and prohibited then why would Allah ﷻ single out the
birthday of Prophet Yahya عليه السلام and Prophet Isa عليه السلام? It
is to be remembered that these are the words of Allah
ﷻ and He is the One who is sending *salaam* on to His
messengers and clearly signifying their birthdays as
peculiar and significant days.

If Allah ﷻ is ordering mankind to convey these
salaams on to Prophet Yahya عليه السلام and Prophet Isa عليه السلام
how can one say it is prohibited to do the same for the
Beloved Prophet Muhammad ﷺ, on his birthday who
is the last and greatest of all Prophets?

A birthday is significant in that a day is singled out
for collective worship. One type of salaam is *salaam
ul aam,* a general one and the other type *salaam ul
qass,* which is sent together collectively. Although we
are encouraged to send *salaat* and *salaam* on Prophet
Muhammad ﷺ, every day, having one day in particular

means a collective act of worship takes place, which is always superior. Indeed *salaam* can also be viewed as a gift from Allah ﷻ to His Prophets' just as we give gifts to each other on our birthdays.

Authentic Tafsir works

To substantiate and elaborate the Qur'anic verses mentioned previously, the tafsir works of reliable and authentic leading *aima*, scholars, will be discussed, with particular reference to Surah Yunus, 10:58.

Imam Alusi in *Ruh ul Ma'ani*, [Vol.2 pg 141] interprets Surah Yunus, [10:58] by quoting a statement of Abdullah ibn Abbas ﷺ, an expert in tafsir. He states that the word *fadl* in Surah Yunus means *ilm*, knowledge, and is a reference to the Qur'an. Since this *ilm* came about as a result of the means of the Prophet ﷺ, who received this Divine revelation, Ibn Abbas ﷺ states that the *rahma* Allah ﷻ refers to in the verse is the Prophet ﷺ, himself. In conclusion he says the coming and raising of this *rahma* in the form of the Prophet ﷺ, is an occasion to be celebrated and rejoiced by all. Imam Alusi then gives many other authorities that also quote the tafsir of Ibn Abbas ﷺ, including Imam Baghdadi and Ibn Sakir, all whom say *rahma* is Prophet Muhammad ﷺ.

Imam Jalal ad-Din Suyuti in *Darr ul Manthur*, [vol. 4 pg. 330] also quotes Ibn Abbas ﷺ and says *fadl* is *ilm*, referring to the Qur'an and *rahma* is Prophet Muhammad ﷺ.

Imam Ibn Hayyan Andalusi, an Imam of the seventh and eighth century utilizes the tafsir of Ibn Abbas ﷺ in *Tafsir Al Bahr ul Muhit*, [vol. 5 pg. 171], which is narrated through Dahhaq (Ibn Abbas' senior student).

Imam Ibn Jawzi also uses the same chain of transmission in, *Zad ul Masir*, [vol.4 pg. 40] after giving various meanings for these two words and implications. He states that although they have different meanings we need to see what it refers to in the context of this verse when Allah ﷻ has asked us to rejoice.

Imam Tabrasi, a great Imam of tafsir from the 6th Century in *Majma ul Bayan*, (vol. 5 pg. 177-178) gives an explanation of this verse. He comments that in reality Allah ﷻ is stating to His Prophet ﷺ, that tell those who rejoice of things of the *dunya*, if they want to rejoice something then they should rejoice in Allah's ﷻ *fadl* and *rahma*, that has been bestowed and sent upon them. He says there are two things to be celebrated, the revelation of the Qur'an, which is Allah's ﷻ *fadl* and the raising of Prophet Muhammad ﷺ, who is the *rahma*. Imam Tabrasi adds that Qatada and Mujadid report it, that Imam Abu Jafar Al Baqir said that Allah's ﷻ *fadl* is the Prophet Muhammad ﷺ. Qatada and Mujahid were the students of Abdullah ibn Abbas ﷺ and Muhammad Al Baqir was the grandson of Imam Hussain ﷺ as he was the son of Imam Zayn-ul-Abideen and also the father of Imam Jafar as-Sadiq.

Earlier in Surah Jumah, it was shown how Allah ﷻ, after praising the Prophet ﷺ and listing his qualities, addresses mankind and states had it not been for the raising of the Prophet ﷺ, man would have remained in error and it is this raising that is the *rahma* and grace of Allah ﷻ.

> "*That is the Grace of Allah, which He bestows on whom He wills. And Allah is the owner of Mighty Grace*". [Qur'an, 62:4]

"*Dhalika fadlullah*" the Grace of Allah has been taken to refer to the Prophet ﷺ, by many scholars of Islam too. In the tafsir of Abdullah ibn Abbas ؓ (*Tanwir ul Miqbas*, pg 471), Ibn Abbas ؓ gives various meanings to this verse and in one he includes the meaning of *fadlil adheem* as being Prophet Muhammad ﷺ, since the Qur'an was revealed on to him.

In his tafsir work *Jalalayn*, Imam Suyuti says, regarding the words *dhalika fadlullah*, Allah's ﷻ *fadl* means the Prophet Muhammad ﷺ and whoever came with him

In the tafsir of Imam Khazin, *Lubab Al Tawil Ma`ani al Tanzil*, [vol. 4 pg. 265] under Surah Jumah verse 4, Allah's ﷻ *fadl* is that He sent His beloved Prophet ﷺ to us and that is a great favour upon us.

Imam Alusi in *Ruh ul Ma'ani* (Part 28, pg. 94- 95) says *dhalika fadlul azeem* is an indication towards the Prophet ﷺ, who came to the unlettered people of this world.

Imam Nasafi in his tafsir, *Madarik Al Tanzil Wa Haqaiq Al Tanzil*, [vol. 4 pg 198] states the coming of the Prophet ﷺ, in this world and being a prophet for all times and centuries is the *fadlullah*, the Grace of Allah ﷻ. Even though future generations will not see him they are entitled to come under the blessing of *falyafrahoo*. Imam Zamakhshari reiterates this in his tafsir work, Al Kashshaf, [vol. 4 pg. 530].

Ibn Kathir in his, *Tafsir al Quran Al Azeem*, [vol. 4 pg. 364] uses similar words, that the *fadl* referred to in the verse is the coming of the Prophet ﷺ, to the *Ummah* and whatever is revealed to him for his *Ummah* is the *fadl* of Allah ﷻ.

Ibn Jawzi in *Zad ul Masir*, [vol. 8 pg. 260] says the Prophet's ﷺ, coming down to mankind and being raised is the *fadl* referred to in Surah Jumah. This is also reiterated by Abu Hayyan Andalusi in his tafsir works [vol. 8 pg. 265] as well as Shaykh Tantawi Jawhari, a modern Egyptian scholar in his book *Al Jawahir fi Tafsir ul Quran*, [Part 24, pg. 174-175].

Shaykh Ahmed al Mustafa al Maraghi in his, *Tafseer al Maraghi*, [vol.10 pg. 96] states Allah's ﷻ great *fadl* upon mankind is the sending of His beloved Prophet ﷺ, who is the sanctifier and purifier of all, providing us with the light of guidance.

Imam Tabrasi in his tafsir work, *Majma ul Bayan*, [vol.10 pg 429] also says Allah ﷻ has said sending His Prophet ﷺ, for now and the future is Allah's ﷻ *fadl* upon us.

Thus it is clear from numerous works of great classical and modern scholars the *fadl* and *rahma* referred to in the Qur'an is indeed a direct reference to our beloved Prophet ﷺ and thus the commandment in Surah Yunus to celebrate the Mercy of the Prophet Muhammad ﷺ, is a direct divine commandment to celebrate the *Mawlid* of Prophet Muhammad ﷺ.

Evidences from the Sunnah

There are many Hadith that provide clear evidences for the legality of celebrating the birth and raising of the Prophet Muhammad ﷺ.

First Hadith

It is reported by Abdullah ibn Abbas ؓ that the Prophet ﷺ, had migrated to Madina and saw the Jews were fasting on the 10th of Muharram, *Yaum e Ashura*. He asked them why they fasted on that day. They replied that this was a spiritual and righteous day; a blessed day since on this day God gave Bani-Israel liberty and independence from Pharaoh. The Prophet ﷺ, then said "If you are fasting on a day when Musa عليه السلام received success on this day (liberation from Pharaoh and his tyrannical government) then I am closer to Musa عليه السلام than you. I have a better right than you over Musa عليه السلام. So I will fast on the same day due to this success, due to Allah's ﷻ blessing on him." So the Prophet ﷺ, ordered his Companions to begin to fast on the day of Ashura. [Sahih Muslim, Book 6, Ch. 19 Hadith no. 2518, 2520]

This is Hadith is also cited in Sahih Bukhari, (vol. 7, Kitab-al-Sawm, Ch. 29, Hadith no.2157 and also in Kitab al Anbiya Ch. 24; in the Muwatta of Imam Malik, Kitab-al-Siyam, Hadith no. 28; in the Musnad of Imam Ahmed bin Hanbal as well as by Imam Asqalani who gives many references in his book "*Fath al Bari*", Vol. 4, pg. 245-249.

This Hadith creates the juristic principle that it is permissible to celebrate a blessing of Allah ﷻ even if it is celebrating an event that took place on a particular day and in this case the blessing conferred onto the people was their liberation from Pharaoh through the means of their Prophet, Musa عليه السلام. When the Prophet ﷺ, heard the answer of the Jews, he did not rebut their celebration, nor did he say it was not permissible to celebrate such a day. Instead he commented that the Muslims had a greater right to celebrate and thus asked the Muslims to fast on this day too.

It is clear from this Hadith that if the day of Ashura was made blessed due to Prophet Musa عليه السلام and the Jews celebrated it out of gratitude to him and Allah ﷻ, then surely the day that the beloved Prophet ﷺ, was made *rahmatalil alimeen* should also be celebrated by us.

Prophet Musa عليه السلام came just for the *Bani-Israel* but Allah ﷻ sent His mercy, in the form of Prophet Muhammad ﷺ, to liberate the whole of mankind from all burdens. The birth of the Prophet ﷺ, came as liberation from every kind of tyranny, cruelty and suppression. It was the day of the birth of justice and the establishment of *haq*, truth and righteousness. So how can we possibly resist in rejoicing and thanking Allah 🕌 for His Mercy on this day.

In another narration of this hadith in Sahih Muslim [Kitab-ul-Sawm, Book 6, Hadith. no.2528], again reported by Ibn Abbas ؓ, he says the Jews, in answering the Prophet's 🕌, question said they held this day with great esteem and regard. So they fasted on the day of Ashura out of respect and reverence, known as *tazeem*. If this is the case then does not the day of the raising and birth of Allah's 🕌 Prophet 🕌, deserve respect and reverence? If we can respect the day Prophet Musa ؑ liberated the Jews then we can surely respect and revere the day the seal of the Prophets' 🕌, was born.

It is sometimes argued that since the Jews celebrated the day of Ashura through keeping a fast, any celebration based upon this Hadith should thus be done just by fasting. Critics argue that in modern times Muslims celebrate the Milad-un-Nabi as an Eid, which has no base in the Sunnah and has its roots in the Asian sub-continent. This however is an erroneous view. The Jews did not celebrate this day just through fasting. This is merely one of the acts that they did. Moreover even if they had only fasted on this day this still cannot detract from the fact that an event took place, which was considered a blessing from Allah 🕌 and the Prophet 🕌, made this blessing worthy of being commemorated, so much so that he made it a part of his Sunnah.

In actual fact the Jews celebrated this day in many ways. The day of Ashura was celebrated as an Eid and considered a great event where even the women were given beautiful dresses and jewellery to wear. In another Hadith of Sahih Muslim, [Kitab-al-Sawm, Book. 6, Hadith no. 2522] Abu Musa ﷺ reported:

> "The day of Ashura was one which the Jews respected and revered and they treated it as an **Eid.** The Messenger of Allah ﷺ, said: You also observe fast on this day."

In another Hadith of Sahih Muslim, [Kitab-al-Sawm, Book. 6, no. 2523], Abu Musa ﷺ reported:

> "The people of Khaybar (most of them were Jews) observed fast on that day of Ashura and they treated it as an Eid and gave their women ornaments and beautiful dresses to wear. The Messenger of Allah ﷺ, said: You observe fast on this day." (Also in Sahih Bukhari Hadith no. 2005)

What is interesting is that the Prophet ﷺ, did not question the celebration of the day as an Eid. He understood why they celebrated the day as an Eid and accepted this fact. He did not question the celebrations or even criticize the buying of new clothes and jewellery, nor did he prohibit the Companions from doing the same or confined them to just fasting. The reason is that this day was already a day of Eid and an accepted fact by all. It was not only the Jews but the Makkans themselves who celebrated this day as an Eid before the migration. This was not similar to the Eid of Shariah, but similar to it in respect of the act of celebration.

Imam Asqalani, in *Fath ul Bari*, [vol.4 p.245] stated that this was the day when the Ka'aba was first dressed and so the Makkans celebrated this day as an Eid. The Prophet ﷺ and the Companions were already celebrating this out of reverence and respect due to the ancient history involved. Imam Asqalani also quotes Abu Hurayrah ﷺ who says that this was the day of Prophet Nuh's عليه السلام boat landing on the mountain of Judi, and thus celebrated for this reason too.

That is why the Prophet ﷺ, did not ask about the Eid festivities but asked regarding the fast. It was only when the Jews began to criticize the Muslims later, did the Prophet ﷺ, ask the Companions to increase their fasts to one day before and one day after. By basing his arguments on this Hadith, Imam ibn Hajar Asqalani establishes the legality of the Mawlid concluding:

> "From this, we learn to perform the act of thankfulness to Allah ﷻ, the Most High on a certain day for a bounty He has bestowed or a disaster He has averted. And that act has to be repeated on the same day every year (anniversary). And thankfulness to Allah ﷻ,

the Most High is done with different kinds of acts of worship like sujud (prostration), fasting, giving charity and recitation (of the Qur'an). And what bounty is greater than the bounty of the coming of the Prophet ﷺ, the one who is the Prophet of Mercy on that day?"

Second Hadith

The Prophet ﷺ, also specified his own birthday in the same way. In a Hadith narrated by Abu Qatada Ansari ﷺ, he reports that Allah's Messenger ﷺ, was asked about fasting on Monday, whereupon he said:

> "It is (the day) when I was born and revelation was sent down to me." [Sahih Muslim, Book 6, Number 2606].

This Hadith is also reported by Imam Bayhaqi in his *Sunan ul Kubra*. [Vol. 4, pg. 300 Hadith no 8182, 8259], in the *Sunan* of Imam Nasai and the *Musnad* of Imam Ahmad bin Hanbal.

It is clear from this Hadith that the Prophet ﷺ, was very happy about the day of his birth and so fasted out of gratitude. Fasting is a form of worship, so one can celebrate this day by any form of worship. One can fast or hold gatherings or provide food to the poor, all being acts of worship.

The third Hadith is regarding a dream seen by Abbas ﷺ, the uncle of the Prophet ﷺ. Before the birth of the Prophet Muhammad ﷺ, his father, Abdullah ﷺ had already passed away, so a lady slave called Thuwayba, was sent to Aminah's house for her help and service. Upon the birth of the Prophet ﷺ. Thuwayba came running to Abu Lahab, the Prophet's, peace be upon, uncle, to give the good news of the birth of his nephew. Abu Lahab became extremely happy and raising two fingers pointed to Thuwayba saying "I free you in thankfulness of the birth of my nephew". That day was a Monday. When he died he came in the dream of Abbas ﷺ who asked him how he was fairing in the life after death. Abu Lahab replied: "I am in the fire of hell day and night and have no escape except Monday. The punishment is reduced for me and from these two fingers of mine I receive water from which I drink (like a fountain) for I freed Thuwayba on the birth of the Prophet ﷺ.

This Hadith is in the Sahih of Imam Bukhari, Kitab-ul-Nikah who quotes this from his own Shaykh, Imam Abdul Razzaq who was the student of Abu Hanifah ﷺ. It is also quoted by Imam Ibn Asqalani, in Fath ul Bari, Ibn Kathir, Imam Bayhaqi, Imam Suhayli, Imam Baghawi, Imam Qurtubi, Imam Jawzi, Imam Mullah Ali Qari, and Imam Abdul Haq Muhaddith Dehlavi.

Abu Lahab was an infidel and one of the greatest enemies of Islam having been cursed in the Qur'an too. Yet despite this he was still given a favour and benefit from his act. It thus stands to reason that if a man such as Abu Lahab can be blessed then surely those Muslims who celebrate the Milad will receive manifold blessings too.

Unfortunately many people use different arguments to criticize this Hadith. Firstly some critics have argued that since it is an Islamic principle that a pious act done by a *kafir* is not rewarded in the Hereafter, how can Abu Lahab benefit? Imam Razzaq discusses this subject in his *Musanaf* [Vol 7 p. 478], as does Imam Abdul Haq Muhaddith Dehlavi. They state that this is the *khasais* (speciality) of the Prophet 變, and an exception just reserved for him. Imam Ibn Kathir in *Sirah al Nabuwa*, [vol. 1 pg 224] states this is because of the *fadl* of the Prophet 變, who is given this exception and is reiterated by Imam Suyuti, Imam Shaybani, Ibn Hashim and Imam Baghawi too. Moreover in a Hadith of Sahih Bukhari the Prophet 變 states that his uncle, Abu Talib will benefit from his intercession, which is again part of the *khasais-e-muhammadiyy* (Speciality of the Prophet 變).

A second criticism levelled at this Hadith is that the event has been narrated in the form of a dream and so loses some of its integrity. This again is not a valid point. This Hadith has been accepted by Imam Bukhari in his Sahih who is one of the greatest muhaddith's so we cannot object to it. If this dream was not to be accepted then why did he accept it? Moreover this is a narration of Abbas 🌼 and if he had considered the dream unimportant then he too would not have narrated it and rejected it as insignificant. Both of these great men as well as the other scholars mentioned earlier all considered the Hadith as authentic and used it in arguments pertaining to the legality of the Mawlid.

A third criticism is that Abbas 🌼 had this dream when he had not accepted Islam and he is quoting something said by another non-Muslim thus querying its authenticity. Again this is not a valid critique. When we take this Hadith as evidence that celebrating the birth of the Prophet 🌼, is rewarded, the base of this argument has no link with the *aqeeda* of Abu Lahab and the information he gives. The evidence is based on the narration of Abbas 🌼. If he was not a Muslim at the time of the dream, he was a Muslim when he reported it. It is part of the *Usul* of Hadith, legal and juristic principles, that the narrator of Hadith must be a Muslim. Abbas 🌼 narrated this dream in his capacity as a Companion of the Prophet 🌼, whilst living in Madinah.

Fourth Hadith

Those critics who argue that only the two Eids of Shariah should be celebrated are also in error. In a Hadith of Sahih Bukhari, [Kitab-al-Iman, Ch. 34, Hadith n.45] a Jew quoted a Quranic verse to Umar 🌼 (*'today we have completed your Deen for you and have chosen the Deen of Islam for you'*) and said had such a verse been revealed to us in our Torah we would have celebrated that day as an Eid day. In this statement there is an implicit question addressed to Umar ﷺ asking why the Muslims did not celebrate this day as an Eid too. Umar ﷺ replied: 'We know which day and which place this verse was revealed on to the Prophet ﷺ, The day of this revelation was Arafah – *Yaum al-hajj* and that was a Friday'.

On this answer Imam Asqalani raises a question. He states that a doubt can emerge in ones mind that the question was not answered satisfactorily. The Jewish man wanted to ask why this day had not been celebrated as an Eid and the answer should have been given in the same way – i.e. we do celebrate it as an Eid or that there are only two Eids in Islam and other Eid celebrations are prohibited. However the answer given by Umar ﷺ does not appear to address the question directly, merely informing the Jew the day upon which the verse was revealed. Imam Asqalani then answers his own question and comments that when Umar (ra] mentioned the day of Hajj and Friday, in fact he was implying that we already celebrate this day as an Eid since *al-hajj* is one of the Eid's of Shariah and every Friday, *Jumma*, is also considered an Eid for Muslims too. He did not reply that celebrating something as an Eid is confined just to certain named days but merely said we already have celebrations on this day. Moreover the Jew did not pose a question again or ask for clarification but kept quiet indicating he understood.

It is thus established from this Hadith that if a verse containing good tidings revealed on to the Prophet ﷺ, is worthy of being celebrated as an Eid then why cannot the day that the Prophet ﷺ, came to this world be celebrated too?

Imam Tirmidhi also reported a similar event in *Kitab Tafseer ul Qur'an* [chap 6, n 3044] from Abdullah ibn Abbas ﷺ. Similar to the one in Sahih Bukhari. He states he recited these verses from Surah Al-Maidah and a Jewish man who was standing near him commented that had this verse been revealed on to them (the Jews) they would have adopted this day as an Eid. Ibn Abbas ﷺ replied, endorsing the idea, saying the Muslims have already made it as a day of two Eids. These verses were revealed on Jumma and on the Day of Arafah meaning the Jews would have celebrated it as one Eid but we celebrate it as a double Eid. Those who argue that we cannot use the word Eid for celebrations are also incorrect since Ibn Abbas ﷺ says *'eidain'* in the Hadith and refers to Friday as *'yaum-ul-eid'*.

The words Yaum ul eid are also contained in a Hadith of Sunan Abu Dawud, (Kitab al Salat, Ch. *fadlal Yaum al jummah*, Hadith no.1043). Here the Prophet ﷺ, said the Ummah should read as much *salaam* and *darood* on him on a Friday in particular, as this is the day of the creation of Prophet Adam ﷺ, the birth or *khalq* of a Prophet being *Yaum ul eid*. The Companions then asked if it would be possible that the *salaam* reaches him after his demise? He replied in the affirmative saying Allah ﷻ has forbidden the earth and land to eat the bodies of the Prophet's.

So if Friday has been singled out as a special day being the day of creation of Prophet Adam عليه السلام, in other words the birthday of the first prophet of Islam, then surely the birthday of the last Prophet ﷺ, should can also be singled out as an Eid.

In another Hadith in the *Sunan* of Imam Nasai, [vol. 1 n.1666 pg. 519, vol.3 pg. 91] the Prophet ﷺ, said we should fire *bakhoor* in mosques as it is the Milad day of Prophet Adam عليه السلام and the day of *darood* for me. [See also the Sunan of Imam Ibn Majah, vol.1, pg. 385 n.1085]. Bakhoor is a special incense that is lighted and releases a beautiful smelling fragrance. Elsewhere the Prophet ﷺ, has also said that on the day of Jumma one must first bathe and wear clean clothes, and then send *darood* on him collectively. Umar ﷺ also appointed a man to perfume the mosques every Friday. [Sunan Imam Abu Dawud Hadith n.1666]

Fifth Hadith

The Prophet ﷺ, himself celebrated his *Milad*. In a Hadith narrated by Anas ﷺ contained in the Sunan of Imam Bayhaqi, [vol.9 p.300 no. 43], [also mentioned by Imam Tabrani, Imam Zahbi, Imam Asqalani in *Fath ul Bari*, and Imam Haythami) states that the Prophet ﷺ,

sacrificed some animals and did an *aqiqa* for himself after the announcement of his Prophethood.

Imam Suyuti, commenting on this Hadith states that this was not an *aqiqa* done in the traditional sense since his grandfather Abdul Muttalib had already done the *aqiqa* of the Prophet ﷺ, seven days after his birth. Since it is not possible to repeat an act of Shariah once it is already done, i.e. one cannot repeat their prayers once they have already been performed, Imam Suyuti states that the reason for the sacrifice of the animals was an act of thankfulness and a celebration performed by the Prophet ﷺ, for his birth. The Prophet ﷺ, was thanking Allah ﷻ for his status as *rahmatalil alimeen*. Imam Suyuti finally concludes it is *mustahab* (advisable) for us to celebrate the Mawlid in *ijtima* (collectively) since the Prophet ﷺ, sacrificed animals and distributed the food and thus we too should have a gathering and distribute food and rejoice in a good manner. [*Husn Maqsid fi `Amal-il Mawlid* by Imam Jalal ad-Din Suyuti, pp. 64-6].

Some critics may argue that since the Prophet's ﷺ, original *aqiqa* was done in the period of *jahiliyyah* he wanted to repeat the *aqiqa* to ensure its proper performance. However this is not a valid argument since if those acts of Shariah performed in the time of *jahiliyyah* needed to be repeated then why were many other similar acts not repeated by the Prophet ﷺ? Why for example did he not repeat his *nikah* to Khadija ؓ, which was originally done 15 years prior to Prophethood? The *nikah* had been read by his uncle Abu Talib and the *mahr* was paid by him too.

Thus it is clearly evident that the *Mawlid* of the Prophet ﷺ, has its origins and roots in the Qur'an and Sunnah and is a celebration that all Muslims should eagerly rejoice in.

PART TWO

The Concept of *Bid'ah*

Dr. Zahid Iqbal

THE CONCEPT OF *BID'AH*

The issue of *Bid'ah* or innovations in religion is a hotly debated one in current times. It has been argued, sometimes with much vigour and polemic that practises in the religion of Islam that were not current at the time of the Prophet , or his companions should be rejected and could even lead to *kufr* or disbelief. It has been the opinion of the vast majority of the *Ulama* throughout the ages that there is *Bid'ah* of two types, that which is permissible, and that which is not. It is the purpose of what is before you to reiterate the correct position, that innovations or newly introduced practises in the Din of Islam can not only be permissible, but also rewarded, hopefully providing clarification to the many people who have been confused about the issue.

The Definition of the word Bid'ah

The word *Bid'ah* in Arabic is derived from the root word *Bada`ah*, literally meaning to create a new thing without precedence. It is synonymous with the word

Khalk that means to create something out of something else. The attributive name *Al Badi* is also derived from the same root to denote Allah ﷻ as the Creator of things that had no previous existence. In the Qur'an Allah ﷻ is *Badi ussamawaati wal ard* i.e. the Creator of the Heavens and Earth (out of nothing). Therefore, in its literal sense, the word *Bid'ah* has no negative connotations; it plainly refers to anything that comes into existence that is novel or not previously known.

In the technical sense, in the way it is used in the Shariah it means an addition to the Din of Islam that was not known or practised at the time of the Prophet ﷺ, or his companions.

The concept of Bid'ah in the Qur'an.

The Qur'an, the primary source of Knowledge in Islam, has a most important proof of the permissibility of beneficial introductions into the Din. In Surah Al-Hadid, Allah ﷻ says:

> "As for monasticism, they invented it themselves, for we had not enjoined it on them, seeking thereby to please Allah; but they did not observe it faithfully. We rewarded only those who were truly faithful, but many of them were transgressors".
> [Qur'an, 57:16]

The word 'invented' used in the above passage is a translation of the Arabic word *Ibtada'uha* which literally means 'they made a *Bid'ah*.' The verse tells us that monasticism (*Rahbaniyat*) was instituted by the followers of the Prophet Isa ﷺ after him as a new act, as a *Bid'ah*, for the purpose of seeking the pleasure of Allah ﷻ. Allah ﷻ does not condemn this act but rather tells us that after its adoption it was not followed properly. It is clear that this verse contains an implied permission granted to them for this new act. If one reads the words carefully, it is apparent that if Allah ﷻ were condemning the new act, then there would be no need to remark that they did not observe it faithfully. Having introduced this new act of monasticism, they should have fulfilled its conditions and requirements to achieve the purpose for which they had adopted in the first place. Instead Allah ﷻ condemns those who, having adopted monasticism, did not perform it in the proper way: *but many of them were transgressors.* In fact not only was the new act permitted, but it was also rewarded, as the verse tells us: *We rewarded only those who were truly faithful.* In the context of the preceding part, this would refer to those who were true believers and fulfilled the conditions of the new act and thus achieving the target of *seeking thereby to please Allah.*

There is an important point to consider here. The practice of monasticism has been abrogated and cancelled in Islam, but the principle contained in this verse of the acceptability of a new act performed with the correct intention and fulfilling certain conditions is not abrogated, but remains. The new practice introduced for the pleasure of Allah ﷻ, in the principles of Islamic jurisprudence becomes a *Bid'ah* of guidance; that which violates the laws of Shariah becomes a *Bid'ah* of misguidance.

The concept of Bid'ah in the Hadith.

It is related from the route of Jarir Ibn Abdullah ﷺ that the Prophet ﷺ, said:

> "*Whosoever introduced a beneficiary action in Islam will be rewarded for his practice as well as for the practice of the people who follow him, without lessening their reward. Whosoever introduced a bad practice in Islam will take the sin for it as well as the sin of the people who follow him, without lessening their sin*". (Muslim).

This hadith, which is of sound classification, is very clear and unambiguous is a foundation for proving the validity of good innovations in Islam. The criterion used as to whether or not a new action is accepted is that it should be *hasanah*, or beneficial. If the action is beneficial then there is an immense reward for it. New introductions that are bad are punished severely. Scholars of Islam, as will be seen later have derived the conditions for a new act to be considered beneficial or bad.

Although the context of this hadith relates to a specific incident during the time of the Prophet 靐, when some companions came forward to offer charity to some poverty-stricken new arrivals at Madinah, the meaning is general. It is not permissible to claim that this Hadith applies only to charity as a general term was used: *Whosoever introduced a beneficiary action in Islam.* The Prophet 靐, did not restrict the reward to 'He who spends in charity.' It is the rule among the scholars of Islam that if an ayah of hadith was revealed for a specific incident or reason yet a general term were used in it then its application would be general and not restricted to that incident.

Some people translate the word *sunnatan* as the specific Sunnah of the Prophet 靐, instead the general word 'action' or 'practice.' In other words, whoever revived a Sunnah of the Prophet 靐, will be rewarded etc. However this is a gross mistranslation of the Hadith. It is impossible to differentiate such a thing as a good Sunnah, as all the practices of the Prophet 靐, were good, and the concept of a 'bad Sunnah' for obvious reasons cannot be entertained at all. Therefore it is impossible for this Hadith to apply to the Sunnah of the Prophet 靐. The authentic Hadith of the Prophet 靐, translated as:

> "*Abstain from innovations, for every kind of innovation is a Bid'ah, and every Bid'ah is misguidance and all misguidance leads to hellfire*"

is often used in an attempt to prove that all new things introduced in Islam are forbidden. This Hadith would apparently contradict with that given above, however one must study the whole Hadith of which this is only a portion, and thus read it in context to the rest. One must also interpret this Hadith according to the other evidence from either the Qur'an or Hadith instead of giving a meaning from our own (mis) understanding. The whole Hadith is:

> I command you to have Taqwa, and to be obedient to those appointed leader over you, even if it be an Abyssinian slave. O my companions, those who live after me will, very soon, see a lot of differences among you. Stick to my path and the path of the Rightly Guided Khalifas. Abstain from innovations, for every kind of innovation is a Bid'ah, and every Bid'ah is misguidance and all misguidance leads to hellfire.

This Hadith is a warning about events to come **very soon** after the Prophet's 鬌, passing on; events characterised by differences among the companions. The Prophet's 鬌, advice was to stick to his path and that of the Rightly Guided *Khalifas*, indicating that there will be differences of opinion against Abu Bakr 鬌, Umar 鬌, Uthman 鬌, and Ali 鬌, and that when these arise, the people should follow them and also the Sunnah of the Prophet 鬌.

In fact, the time immediately after the death of the Prophet 🕮, was a time of great disruption and tribulation for the Muslims. There came several people claiming to be prophets after the Prophet Muhammad's 🕮, who fought against Abu Bakr ﷺ. There were groups of Muslims, who denied the paying of *Zakah*, and there were people who abandoned Islam and challenged the authority of the Prophet 🕮, becoming apostates. Abu Bakr ﷺ said he would fight those people who claimed to be prophets, who did not pay Zakah or became apostates. After him came people who denied the Khalifate of Uthman ﷺ, and that of Ali ﷺ. The *Khwarij* sect came about which fought against Ali ﷺ. In all, it was an extremely volatile time. It is clear that the 'innovations' mentioned in this Hadith refer to major disruptions that occurred, including people declaring Prophethood after the Prophet 🕮, people denying the paying of Zakah, and the distorted beliefs of the *Khwarij*. These were the kinds of 'innovation' referred to by the Prophet 🕮 that were misguidance and therefore leading to Hellfire.

Further evidence for this comes from another sound Hadith related by Ibn Abbas ﷺ. The word 'innovation' used in the Hadith quoted above is a translation of the word *Muhdasa*, which is derived from the word *Ihdas*, meaning disruption. The following Hadith gives us the Prophet's 🕮, interpretation of this word:

"O people, you will be gathered on the Day of Judgement in the same way you were born (naked). The first person to be given the dress of the hereafter will be Prophet Ibrahim. Some people from my Ummah will be brought in front of me, and taken toward hell. I will recognise them and I will say, "These are my companions." An angel will say, "Don't you know what kinds of disruption (Ihdasa) they committed after you? Although they embraced Islam in your life, soon after your demise they became apostates and turned towards kufr".

This Hadith of the Prophet ﷺ, therefore defines what sort of innovation in the Din of Islam is a misguidance, that is something major in the fundamentals or belief system of Islam, typical of those innovations that occurred not long after his time. This argument enables us to understand the following Hadith:

"He who innovates something in this matter of ours that is not of it will have it rejected". (Agreed)

The same word *Ahdasa* is used here which is translated as 'innovates.' Using the hadith about the companions sent to Hellfire who committed grave disruptions to interpret the word *Ahdasa*, the Hadith is also referring to major additions or alterations to the

Din of Islam, **that are not of it**. Another variation of this Hadith related by Muslim is as follows:

"He who does an act which our matter is not (in agreement) with, will have it rejected".

This Hadith gives us a criterion by which every new act must be judged, namely that it should not go against the Shariah and be compatible with the Qur'an and Sunnah. Therefore every new act is not condemned but rather should be evaluated on its merits to see whether it is in agreement with the Qur'an and Sunnah.

A final point regarding the interpretation of Hadith needs to be mentioned. If interpretation is attempted without proper knowledge, one may find apparent contradictions between various Hadith. If one interpreted the last few Hadith as meaning every new act in Islam is a misguidance, this would be in contradiction to the first hadith mentioned about the rewards of introducing beneficial practises into Islam and the punishments for introducing bad practises. All the Hadith mentioned above are of sound classification; in reality, there are no contradictions if the Hadith are interpreted properly. This is what the great Scholars of Islam have done. By interpreting correctly and with proper knowledge, they have conformed and bridged the meanings between the Hadith. This concept is very well known in the science of Hadith exegesis; for example, *takhsis al-amm* is a frequent procedure of *usul al-fiqh* by which an apparently unqualified statement is qualified to avoid the contradiction of another necessary principle.

The concept of Bid'ah according to Scholars of Islam.

The vast majority of the classical Scholars of Islam make a distinction between innovations that are acceptable, that may be called innovations of guidance, and those that are not, that may be called innovations of misguidance.

Imam ash-Shafi' wrote, "There are two kinds of introduced matters. One is that which contradicts a text of the Qur'an, or the Sunnah, or a report from the early Muslims, or the consensus of the Muslims: this is an innovation of misguidance (*bid'at dalala*). The second kind is that which is in itself good and entails no contradiction of any of these authorities: this is a 'non-reprehensible innovation' (*bid'a ghayr madhmuma*)." [Ibn Asakir, *Tabyin Khadib al-Muftari* (Damascus, 1347), 97, tr. Abdul Hakim Murad]

Similar definitions have been expounded by other great classical scholars, such as Imam al-Bayhaqi, Imam an-Nawawi, and Ibn Abdus-Salaam and Ibn Hajar al-Asqalani, among others.

Ibn Abdus-Salaam (one of the greatest mujtahids) categorised innovations into five types: the obligatory (*wajib*), the recommended (*mandub*), the permissible (*mubah*), the offensive (*makruh*), and the forbidden (*haram*). [Muhammad al-Jurdani, *al-Jawahir al-lu'lu'iyyah fi sharh al-Arba'in al- Nawawiya* (Damascus, 1328), 220-1.]

Among the obligatory innovations Ibn Abdus-Salaam cites the following examples: recording the Qur'an and the laws of Islam in writing at a time when it was feared they would be lost, studying Arabic Grammar in order to resolve controversies over the Qur'an, and developing philosophical theology (*kalam*) to refute the claims of the *Mu'tazilites*. Under recommended innovation come activities such as building *madrassas*, writing books on beneficial Islamic subjects, and in-depth studies of Arabic linguistics. Permissible innovations include worldly activities such as sifting flour, and constructing houses in various styles not known in Madinah. Reprehensible innovations include over decorating mosques or the Qur'an. The category of forbidden innovations includes unlawful taxes, giving judgeships to those unqualified to hold them, and sectarian beliefs and practices that explicitly contravene the known principles of the Qur'an and Sunnah.

Innovations of Guidance and Innovations of Misguidance.

With the concept of *Bid'ah* being clarified somewhat, the reader may want to know what practices fall with the domains of innovations of guidance, which are permissible and rewarded, and innovations of misguidance, which are forbidden and punishable. For innovations of guidance, it would be fair to say that every single Muslim practices these innovations, knowingly or otherwise, and the list is long. A few examples have been mentioned above.

For examples of innovations of misguidance it would be useful to look at the aforementioned Hadith about *Bid'ah* referring to the time soon after the death of the Prophet ﷺ, when there came false prophets, apostates and people who did not pay Zakah. Therefore, if one were to declare or follow another prophet after the Prophet Muhammad ﷺ, this would be an innovation of misguidance. Following on from this, any change in the major beliefs and tenets of Islam would be in the same category. This could include for example, denying the attributes of Allah ﷻ, denying the existence of angels etc.

Any change in the basic practises of Islam would also be an innovation of misguidance, such as reducing or increasing the number of *salah* in a day or changing the number of *rakah*, fasting on forbidden days. Decreeing those things that are *Halaal* as *Haraam* or vice versa would also be an innovation of misguidance as would be adding verses to the Qur'an or falsifying Hadith. As can be seen these are major sins and lead to *Shirk* and even *Kufr*. These things are not necessarily far-fetched, as they seem as the history of Islam bears witness to a number of stray sects of Islam that adopted certain of these practices and beliefs.

There is an often repeated concept held by some Muslims today, that any practice in religion that was not done by the Prophet 🕌, or his companions should be rejected as it is a misguidance and therefore punishable in Hellfire. However one must go beyond slogans and oversimplifications and reach a correct opinion by examining the facts based upon the Qur'an and Sunnah.

As we have seen, new practices are not rejected, but are accepted and even rewarded. However, the practice concerned should be compatible with the dictates of the Shariah, otherwise it will be rejected. The opinion of those who condemn any new act without qualification comes from a misunderstanding of the sources of the Qur'an and Hadith, for example by quoting passages out of context or without the true meaning.

It is apparent that the classical scholars, who probably had a greater knowledge of Qur'anic or Hadith exegesis than any living person today decreed that newly introduced practices are allowed as long as they do not contradict the Qur'an or Sunnah. This stands in marked contrast to the opinion of many so-called learned people today. They should be careful of condemning an act as *Haraam* or prohibited if the Qur'an or Sunnah does not specifically prohibit it, as judging a permissible act as *Haraam* may lead to *Shirk*. In fact, the introduction of new things into the din ensures that Islam can apply itself to any given time and situation, and some new things have even been essential for its preservation and propagation.

The Significance of Chain of Authority

The Significance of Chain of Authority

Imam Muslim in the preface (Muqadimma) of his as-Sahih has entitled a chapter, "Narration from a Reliable Authority is Mandatory in Shariah and Science of Hadith in Order to Eliminate Any Doubt of Perjury in Narrating Knowledge from the Holy Prophet (saw)". Following this, Imam Muslim entitled another chapter, "Declaration of the Fact that the Chain of Authority is Part of the Deen and there should be no Narration Except from a Reliable Chain of Authority".

Imam Muslim also reports from Imam Muhammad bin Sireen (through his own chain), who states, "The science of chain of authority and narration of Hadith is deen itself. You should check whom you are receiving your deen from" (Sahih Muslim Muq:26). He (Imam Ibn Sireen) again states, "Before the fitnah of fabrication of Hadith (and innovation - bida) we never felt any necessity to ask about the chain because all authorities before the period of fitnah were undoubtedly reliable. After this fitnah of fabrication had occurred we started asking the narrator to mention their chain of authority before us; and if the knowledge of deen was narrated from an authority belonging to ahl-us-sunnah we used to accept his transmission; and if he belonged to ahl-ul-bida we rejected it" (Sahih Muslim Muq: 27).

Sa'd bin Ibrahim narrates through Sufyan bin Uyaynah, "Nobody should narrate the knowledge of Rasul Allah (saw) except the reliable authorities". Furthermore, Imam Muslim quotes from Amir ul Mu'mineen fil Hadith Abdullah bin Mubarak, who states, "Al- Isnaad (quoting the chain of authority) is a necessary part of deen. If there was no chain of authority then everyone would have said whatever he wanted to say" (Sahih Muslim Muq: 31).

Imam Muslim elaborated further from Imam Abdullah bin Mubarak, who says, "Between us and between the people who receive from us there are pillars of reliance and these are the chains of authority" (Sahih Muslim Muq:32).

The significance of the chain of transmitters and authorities can be further illustrated through the statement of Imam Ibn Maajah (one of the six great Imams of Sihah Sittah). He has reported a Hadith on the reality of Iman in the preface of his Sunan Ibn Maajah (the same has been reported by Imam Tabarani and Imam Bayhaqi), whereby he narrates from Abus-Sult al-Harawi continuously up to the Holy Prophet (saw) through Sayyidena Ali bin Abi Talib. At the end of the text of Hadith he quotes, "If this isnad (chain of transmitters and authorities) is read upon a person who is insane (majnun) he will certainly be cured." Here lie the blessings (barakah) of the names of the blessed persons who belong to ahl-ul-bayt-an-nabawi and all of them are the Imams of wilayah (sainthood).

Although the words of the Holy Prophet (saw) are always contained in the text of Hadith and not in the chain of authorities, the chain of authorities only consists of the names of reliable persons who are the blessed transmitters. Imam Ibn Maajah has not directed towards reading the text of the Hadith upon an insane person, but has rather emphasized reading the names of the transmitters, which is the chain of authorities; just invoking the names on a patient has become a spiritual treatment. This is the aqeeda of Imam Ibn Maajah, Imam Tabarani and Imam Bayhaqi; the same has been mentioned by Imam Suyuti, as well as by Imam Ibn-ul-Qayyum, the great and famous student of Allama Ibn Taymiyyah.

According to all of these authoritative statements of the Imams, who are the real transmitters of the deen and knowledge of Hadith to us, it is clear and evident that before the substance and content one is inevitably supposed to rely on the chain and authority - these are the people who narrated the knowledge of the deen. If they are proven to be reliable it is only then one would have access to the acceptance of substance and contents of the Hadith. Rather than place emphasis on the text, they have given all the importance to the chain. In any Hadith the text is known as the matan and the chain of authority is known as the sanad or isnaad. The text contains the message of Islam and the teachings of the Holy Prophet (saw), the substance of the Shariah and the Sunnah, whereas the chain consists of personalities. Reliance has been placed on the personalities over the actual content. The Imams have declared the chain of these reliable personalities as a part of deen. Here lies the significance of personalities in Islam - they are the real transmitters of the deen from the Holy Prophet (saw) that is why the Holy Prophet (saw) declared them to be his khulafaa. The companions asked, "Who are the khulafaa?" He replied, "Those who revive my sunnah and are the transmitters of my knowledge to the Ummah" (Ibn Asakir, reported by Imam Hassan bin Ali). That is why the Holy Qur'an in Surah Fatiha has commanded us to follow the footsteps of the blessed personalities in order to achieve al-Hidayah (guidance) and to beseech, "Lead us to the straight path, the path of those (personalities) whom you blessed'. Reliable and blessed personalities have been declared to be symbols of al-Hidayah and it has been made compulsory to identify and follow them. On the other hand some people have been made symbols of misguidance and the wrath of Allah (swt). The Qur'an has commanded us neither to follow them nor to be in their company. As stated in Surah Fatiha, "Not those who gained your wrath, and not those who stood misguided." The Holy Qur'an has defined the "blessed people" in Surah al-Nisa: "The blessed people are the Prophets (an-nabiyyeen), the Truthful (as-Siddiqeen), and the Witnesses (of Truth) (as-Shuhadaa), and the Pious ones (possessing Allah's nearness - as-Saliheen)."

We who belong to Minhaj-ul-Quran are fortunate that we are connected to one of the chosen and blessed people of the Holy Prophet (saw) whom he declared to be one of the community of his khulafaa (vicegerents), Shaykh-ul-Islam Dr Muhammad Tahir-ul-Qadri, the man of reliable authority, one of the great authentic transmitters of the Prophet's (saw) knowledge to the Ummah; from whom scholars of East and West, both Arab and non-Arab, have derived benefit, who come to him to receive ijazah (permission) and isnaad (authority) as an Iman of 'ilm in this century. He is the one who received his permission and authority from the greatest scholars of their time and he delivers his permission and authority to hundreds of great scholars of his time. Being the author of one thousand books and a transmitter of the Holy Prophet (saw) through five thousand orations and narrations, he has revived numerous Islamic sciences, including aqeeda, 'ilm al fiqh, tasawwuf, and ideology through his reconstructive efforts of Islamic thought and philosophy in the modern age. He is the revivalist of the present century. As the Holy Prophet (saw) stated, reported by Abu Hurayah (ra), "Indeed He (Allah) raises in the Ummah at the beginning of every Islamic century one that revives the deen for this Ummah." (Abu Daud, Al-Hakim, Al-Tabarani). The scholars and authorities serving the deen of the Prophet (saw) are in the hundreds and thousands according to their position and status, but the mujaddid is only one in a century; if there is to be another he will be in another part of the world. Shaykh-ul-Islam, was born in 1370 (A.H) and started his revivalist work in 1401 (A.H.), exactly at the beginning of the 15th Islamic century, by founding Minhaj-ul-Quran.

The door of Prophethood has been completely closed in all respects and no Prophet will ever come after the raising of the Holy Prophet (saw) himself. The Prophet (saw) stated that before him every Prophet used to succeed another; with his raising, the chain of Prophethood closed. From now he will be succeeded by the khulafaa (Bukhari and Muslim). The khulafaa are the mujaddideen, awliya, and the ualama-isaliheen.

The mujadideen are the revivalists and the others are the transmitters; while the rest are just preachers. As for the mujaddid, he receives blessings directly from the Holy Prophet (saw) in addition to his other chains of receiving knowledge.

A Hadith of the Holy Prophet (saw) reported through Sa'eed bin Musayyab, which is quoted by Imam ibn Abdil Barr, indicates that the transmitter of knowledge who revives the deen is the direct recipient of blessings of the Prophets and spiritually linked with them.

We are fortunate to be linked with one of those blessed authorities and to enable ourselves to receive the blessings of the Prophet (saw) through his Eminence. Here is presented the chain of authority of Shaykh-ul-Islam, which he receives from his Shuyukh, and upon which he bases his reliance of authority of transmitting the deen to those who are sufficiently qualified and knowledgeable.

His Eminence Shaykh-ul-Islam, Dr Muhammad Tahir-ul-Qadri has received a large number of authorities (Asaneed) and permissions (Ijazaat) for the transmission of knowledge of Hadith, Tafsir, Fiqh, Tasawwuf and other classical Islamic Sciences from numerous great pillars of the Muslim world, widely acknowledged as the fountains of Islamic knowledge in the last century. Some of these are as below:

1. The authorities of his Eminence Shaykh-ul-Islam of the Shuyukh of Al-HARAMAYN (MAKKA and MADINA) are as follows:

- Al-Imam Umar bin Hamadan al-Mahresi,
- Al-Imam Muhammad bin Ali bin Zahir al-Watri
- Al-Imam Ahmad bin Isma'eel al-Barzanji
- Al-Imam Ahmad bin Muhammad as-Sanosi al-Madani
- Al-Imam Ahmad bin Zayni ad-Dahlan

THROUGH:

i. Ash-Shaykh Alawi bin Abbas al-Maliki al-Makki (father of Ash-Shaykh Muhammad bin Alawi al-Maliki al-Makki)
ii. Ash-Shaykh al-Mu'ammar Zia-ud-Din al-Qadri al-Madani' (who died at the age of more than 100 years)
iii. Ash-Shaykh Muhammad bin Alawi al-Maliki al-Makki
iv. Ash-Shaykh Fareed-ud-Din al-Qadri (father of his Eminence

Shaykh-ul-Islam)

2. The authorities of his Eminence Shaykh-ul-Islam of the Shuyukh of BAGHDAD are as follows:

- Al-Imam Abdur-Rahman bin Ali an-Naqeeb al-Baghdadi, (Hujjat-ul--Muhadditheen of his time)
- Al-Imam Abdus-Salam al-Muhaddith al-Aafandi al-Bazzaz Up to Al-Imam Mahmud bin Abdullah al-Aalusi (author of Tafseer Rooh-ul-M'aani)

THROUGH:

i) Ash-Shaykh as-Sayyid Tahir Alauddin al Jilani al-Baghdadi
ii) Ash-Shaykh Fareed-ud-Din al-Qadri (father of his eminence Shaykh-ul-Islam).
Through:

Ash-Shaykh-as-Sayyid Ibraheem Sayf-ud-Din an-Naqeeb al-Baghdadi, Ash-Shaykh Abdul Baqi al-Ansari al-Muhaddith al-Lakhnawi al-Madani,Ash-Shaykh Alawi bin Abbas al-Maliki al-Makki.

3. The authorities of his Eminence Shaykh-ul-Islam of the Shuyukh of ASH-SHAM (SYRIA) are as follows:

- Muhaddith-us-Sham al-Imam Muhmmad Badr-ud-Din bin Yusuf al-Hasani
- Al-Imam Muhammad bin Muhammad bin Ja'far al-Makki al-Kittani
- Al-Imam Abul-Makarim Muhammad Amin Suwayd ad-Damashqi
- Al-Imam Abdul Hayye bin Abdul Kabeer al-Kittani

THROUGH:

i) Ash-Shaykh Muhammad al-Fateh al-Kittani
ii) Ash-Shaykh Fareed-ud-Din al-Qadri (father of his Eminence

Shaykh-ul-Islam) through Ash-Shaykh Muhammad al-Makki al-Kit-tani

4. The authorities of his Eminence Shaykh-ul-Islam of the Shuyukh of LEBANON and TARABULUS are as follows:

- Al-Imam Yusuf bin Isma`eel an-Nabhani (Imam-ul-Muhadditheen of the last century and grandfather of Taqiuddin an-Nabhani)
- Al-Imam Abdul Qadir al-Shalabi at-Tarabalusi

THROUGH:

i) Ash-Shaykh Husayn bin Ahmad Usayran (who died on July 12th 2005 at the age of 98, Lebanon)
ii) Ash-Shaykh Muhammad al-Fateh al-Kittani (Damascus)

5. The authorities of his Eminence Shaykh-ul-Islam of the Shuyukh of Al-MAGHREB and ASH-SHANQEET (MAURITANIA) are as follows:

- Al-Imam al-Arabi al-Azzuzi al-Fasi
- Al-Imam Muhammad bin Mustafa Maa-ul-Aynayn Ash-Shanqeeti
- Al-Imam Abdullah bin Siddique al-Ghimari al-Maghrebi

THROUGH:

i) Ash-Shaykh Husayn bin Ahmad Usayran
ii) Ash-Shaykh As-Sayyid Muhammad al-Fateh al-Kittani
iii) Ash-Shaykh Fareed-ud-Din al-Qadri (father of his eminence Shaykh-ul-Islam) through Ash-Shaykh Muhammad al-Makki al-Kit-tani

6. The authorities of his Eminence Shaykh-ul-Islam of the Shuyukh of HADRAMOT (YEMEN) are as follows:

- Ash-Shaykh al-Habeeb Hamza bin Umar al-Eidrus al-Habashi
- Ash-Shaykh al-Habeeb Ali bin Abdur Rahman al-Habashi

59

- Ash-Shaykh Abdul Qadir bin Ahmad as-Saqqaf
- Ash-Shaykh Abdullah bin Ahmad al-Haddar
- Ash-Shaykh Hasan bin Ahmad al-Ahdal al-Yamani
- Ash-Shaykh Muhammad bin Yahya al-Ahdal al-Yamani
- Ash-Shaykh Isma`eel al-Yamani (author of Nafas-ur-Rahman)

THROUGH:

i. Ash-Shaykh Muhammad bin Alawi al-Maliki al-Makki
ii. Ash-Shaykh Fareed-ud-Din al-Qadri (father of his Eminence Shaykh-ul-Islam) through Ash-Shaykh Alawi bin Abbas al-Maliki al-Makki (father of Shaykh Muhammad bin Alawi al-Maliki al-Makki)

7. The authorities of his Eminence Shaykh-ul-Islam of the Shuyukh of AL-HIND (INDIA AND PAKISTAN) are as follows:

- Al-Imam Ahmad Raza Khan al-Muhaddith al-Faqeeh al-Barelwi
- Al-Imam Ahmad Ali al-Muhaddith As-Saharanpuri
- Al-Imam Abul-Hasanat Abul Hayye bin Abdul Haleem al-Muhaddith al-Lakhnawi (Grand Faqeeh-ul-Hind and Shaykh of Arab and Ajam)
- Al-Imam Abdul Baqi bin Ali al-Ansari al-Lakhnawi al-Madani (up to al-Imam Ash-Shah Wali-Ullah al-Muhaddith ad-Dehlawi)
- AI-Imam Irshad Husayn al-Muhaddith ar-Rampuri
- Al-Imam Ash-Shah Imdad-Ullah al-Muhajir al-Makki (a great Saint and Shaykh of Maulana Ashraf Ali Thanawi, Maulana Rasheed Ahmad Gangohi, Maulana Muhammad Qasim Nanotawi and many others)
- Al-Imam Fad-ul-Haq al-Khayrabadi
- Ash-Shaykh as-Sayyid Didar Ali Ash-Shah al-Muhaddith al-Alwari
- Ash-Shaykh Muhammad Anwar Ash-Shah al-Muhaddith al-Kash-miri (authorof Fayz-ul-Bari)
- Ash-Shaykh Abdush Shakoor al-Muhajir al-Madani
- Ash-Shaykh Muhammad Badr-ul-Alam al-Mirathi

THROUGH:

i) Ash-Shaykh al-Mu'ammar Zia-ud-Din al-Qadri al-Madani (who died at theage of over 100)

ii) Ash-Shaykh as-Sayyid Abdul Ma'bud al Jilani (who died at the age of 165 and was a direct student of Al-Imam Ash-Shah Imdad-Ullah al-Muhajir al-Makki)

iii) Al-Muhaddith-ul-A'azam Ash-Shaykh Sardar Ahmad al-Qadri

iv) Ash-Shaykh as-Sayyid Ahmad Abul-Barakat al-Muhaddith al- Al-wari (Lahori)

v) Ash-Shaykh as-Sayyid Ahmad Saeed a]-Kazimi al-Amrohi

vi) Ash-Shaykh Fareed-ud-Din al-Qadri (father of his Eminence Shaykh-ul-Islam)

vii) Ash-Shaykh Abdur Rashid bin Qutbuddin al-Qadri al-Razavi

viii) Ash-Shaykh Burhan Ahmad al-Farooqi

Listed below are some of the names of the renowned Scholars and Mashaikh of the Islamic World who received permissions (Ijazaat) and authorities (Asaaneed) from his Eminence Shaykh-ul-Islam of the transmission of the Knowledge of Hadeeth, Fiqh and other sciences of Shariah:

1. Ash-Shaykh As`ad Muhammad Sa`eed as-Saghargee, Damascus, Syria (a highly regarded authority in Uloom-ul-Hadith and Fiqh and the author of many renowned books).

2. Ash-Shaykh Abul Khayr ash-Shukri, Damascus, Syria (a well known Scholar and Khateeb of al-Jame'al-Umawi and head of al Jamiyyah al-Muhaddith-ul-Akbar, Syria)

3. Ash-Shaykh Dr Abdur Razzaq Assa'di, Baghdad, Iraq (a well known scholar and author of renowned books and former secretary general of al-Mu'tamar al-Aalmi al-Islami,Iraq)

4. Ash-Shaykh Abdul Wahab Al Mash'hadani, Baghdad, Iraq (a well known Scholar and an author of many books on al-fiqh-ul-Hanafi)

5. Ash-Shaykh Muhammad Amin ash-Shareef (Head of the Faculty of Hadeeth, al-Jamia an-Nizamia, Hayderabad Daccan, India)

6. Ash-Shaykh Hamdoon Ahmad Bin Abdur Raheem, Egypt,(one of the Egyptian Learned Graduates of Jamia Al AZhar)

7. Ash-Shaykh Abdul Muqtadir Bin Muhammad Alwan, Egypt,(one of the Egyptian Learned Graduates of Jamia Al-Azhar)

8. Ash-Shaykh Yousuf bin Younus Ahmad Abdur Raheem, Egypt,(one of the Egyptian Learned Graduates of jamia Al Azhar

9. Ash-Shaykh Hameed Mahmood bin Ahmad Mahmood, Egypt, (one of the Egyptian Learned Graduates of jamia Al Azhar

10. Ahmad Abdullah Muhammad al Jeyad, Egypt,(one of the Egyptian Learned Graduates of jamia Al Azhar

11. Ash-Shaykh Abdul Wahid Yousuf bin Muhammad Mata, Egypt,(one of the Egyptian Learned Graduates of Jamia Al Azhar

12. Assayyid Waseem Al Habbal, Lebanon,(a learned scholar on Islamic fiqh)

Finally, the most unprecedented, unique, highly blessed and honored chain of authority that his Eminence Shaykh-ul-Islam possesses is through only four Shuyukh between Shaykh-ul-Islam and the Great Imams listed below:

- Sayyedena Ghous-ul-Azam As-Shaykh Abdul Qadir al Jilani al-Hasani al-Husayni (Baghdad)
- Al-Imam Ash-Shaykh-ul-Akbar Mohyuddin-ibn-ul-Arabi (author of al-Futuhaat-ul-Makkiyyah) (Damascus)
- Al-Imam Ibn-i-Hajar-al-Asqalani, the greatest authority on Hadeeth (Egypt)

His Eminence Shaykh-ul-Islam's continuous chain of authority (Isnad) up to the above mentioned Great Imams is as under:

Shaykh-ul-Islam narrates (with direct permission and authority) from Ash-Shaykh Husayn bin Ahmad Usayran (Lebanon) who narrates from Ash-Shaykh Abdul Hayye bin Shaykh Abdul Kabeer-al-Kittani who narrates from As-Shaykh al-Mu`ammar Abdul Hadee bin al-Arabi al-Awwad who narrates from al-Imam As-Sayyid Abdul Azziz al-Hafeed al-Habashi. (He was born in 581 (Hijra) and died in 1276 (Hijra) and lived up to 695 years WHO directly studied under and narrated from:

- Al-Imam Abdur Razzaq al-Jilani bin Sayyidina Ghous-ul-Azam al-Jilani from his father at Baghdad
 Al-Imam Ash-Shaykh-ul-Akbar Mohyuddin-ibn-ul-Arabi at Damascus
- Al-Imam -i-Hajar al-Asqalani at Egypt.

His Eminence Shaykh-ul-Islam has received the same authority and Ijaazah of transmission from another chain. His Eminence narrates:

From Ash-Shaykh Husayn bin Ahmad Usayran who narrates from Ash-Shaykh as-Sayyid Ahmad bin Muhammad as-Sanosi al-Madani who narrates from Ash-Shaykh as-Sayyid Muhammad bin Muhammad as-Sanosi Who narrates from Ash-Shaykh as-Sayyid Muhammad bin Ali as-Sanosi who narrates from Al-Imam Abdul Aziz al-Hafeed al-Habashi who received from all of the above mentioned three Great Imams.